About Swedish

Traditional Swedish Weaving, also known as Huck Weaving, became popular in America in the 1940's when crafters used embroidery floss to decorate the borders of huck towels. Today, Swedish Weave stitching can also be used to make table runners, afghans, pillows, placemats, cards and more.

Swedish Weaving is distinguishable in a couple of ways. The stitching only shows on the front of the fabric and when you turn the fabric over, the floss does not show on the back. Traditional Swedish Weave designs are usually mirror images, both top to bottom and side to side.

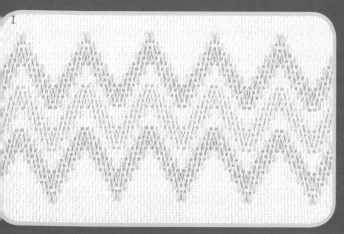

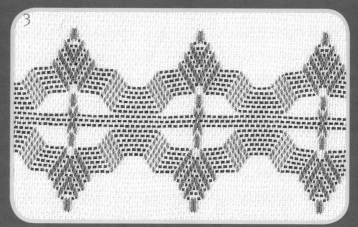

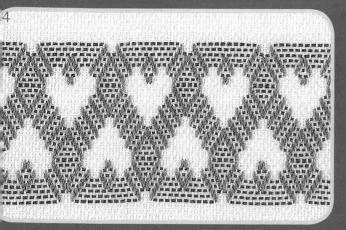

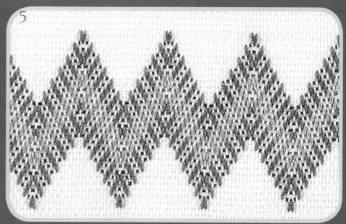

LEISURE ARTS, INC., Maumelle, AR

═ Materials ═

There are only a few things you will need to purchase to make your towel. These items may be found at your local needlework or craft store.

Fabric

The special fabric for these towels is called Huck Toweling. It is a 100% cotton fabric that is 14"-16" wide and sold by the yard. It is easily recognized by the "floats" that are very apparent on the right side of the fabric. Floats are two vertical or horizontal threads that run throughout the fabric; running embroidery floss under these floats allows you to create designs. Due to shrinkage, you will need to purchase ¾ of a yard of fabric for each 24" long finished towel.

Needle

Use a #24 tapestry needle for your stitching. It will slide under the floats easily. The eye is large enough to accommodate six strands of embroidery floss.

Embroidery Floss

Use six strands of DMC embroidery floss as it comes off the skein; it is not necessary to separate the strands and realign them.

Ruler and Water Soluble Fabric Marking Pen

Use a ruler and fabric marking pen to determine your starting point on your towel.

═ Stitching Your Design ═

1. Cut your towel fabric 27" long. Wash the fabric in hot water, dry thoroughly, and press fabric flat.

2. If you would prefer hemmed side edges, turn the side edges of the towel ½" to the wrong side and machine stitch.

3. To find the center of your towel, fold fabric in half lengthwise. On the fold, use the fabric marking pen to make a dot 3" from the bottom of the towel. The center of Row 1 on the chart is marked with an arrow. Your dot corresponds to this arrow; this is where you will begin stitching. You always begin stitching in the center of Row 1 on any of our patterns.

4. Cut embroidery floss to length as specified for Row 1. Thread needle with floss and pull floss through the first vertical float as shown on the chart. Continue pulling your floss through the float until you have an even length of floss on both sides of float. Each row of stitching will begin this way, in the center of the fabric, with floss even on both sides of the float. Stitching is always worked from right to left.

. Following chart and working from right to left, run your needle and floss through floats as shown on the chart and referring to Stitch Diagrams (pg. 4) as necessary. Continue stitching, working the established pattern, until you reach the side edge of the towel. Do not cut floss ends.

. Rotate fabric 180° and rethread needle. Follow chart to complete stitching to opposite edge of towel, again working from right to left. Do not cut floss ends.

. Cut embroidery floss to length as specified for each row. Follow chart to stitch design, always beginning at the center of the row and working right to left. Do not cut floss ends.

═══ Finishing Towel Sides ═══

fter all rows are stitched, it is important to secure your embroidery floss ends. There e three ways to secure the floss ends on the side edges of your towel.

The traditional way to secure floss at the end of a row is to pick up a single thread at the edge of the towel and then run your needle and floss back through the floats, under the last few stitches you worked. Then clip the floss as close as possible to the towel.

The quickest and easiest method is to run your needle and floss through the fabric threads that make up the selvage edge of the toweling fabric. Clip your excess floss as close to the towel as possible.

If you hemmed the side edges of your towel, run the needle and floss through the fabric and come out at the side edge of the towel. Once you have done this with all of your floss ends, machine stitch from top to bottom of towel approximately 1/4" from side edges. Clip floss ends as close as possible to towel.

═══ Finishing Towel Bottom and Top ═══

ou can either hem or fringe the top and bottom of your towel.

To hem your towel, turn top and bottom edges 1/2" to back and machine stitch 1/4" from edge.

To fringe your towel, machine stitch across towel 1/2" to 3/4" from top and bottom edges. Remove horizontal fabric threads up to the machine stitching line.

═ Stitches ═

With all stitches you will enter the float from right to left unless instructed to do otherwise.

Straight Stitch

This is the basic stitch and is done by going over the horizontal floats and under the vertical floats.

Diagonal Straight Stitch

This stitch is identical to the straight stitch except that you stitch at an angle either up or down.

Slant Stitch

With this stitch, bring the needle under the float and go to the float directly above or below. This stitch goes up (slant stitch up) or down (slant stitch down) as pattern indicates.

Half Figure 8

With this stitch, bring the needle under the float and go up or down to the float directly above or below it. <u>Enter</u> that float from the <u>left</u>, bring it through the float then exit on the right. Bring the needle back through the

original float and enter from the right and exit to the left of the float.

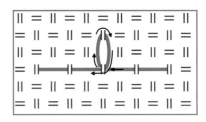

Full Figure 8

With this stitch, go through the float entering right and exiting left. Then go to the float directly above the original float and draw the needle through that float from the <u>left</u> to the right. Come down and go through the original float again. Go to the float directly below the original float and bring the needle through that float going from <u>left</u> to right. Bring the needle back to the original float and enter from the right and exit on the left.

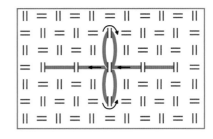

Split Float

With this stitch, bring needle through the right thread of the float exiting in the <u>center</u> of the float. Take your needle to the float directly above or below the original float and draw your needle completely through that float, from right to left. Bring your needle back to the original float and through the second (left) thread of that float again from right to left.

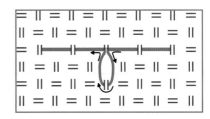

Read General Instructions, pgs. 2-4, before beginning project. Continue stitching in established pattern to edges of towel.

━━ DMC 743 — 1 skein required

══ DMC 744 — 1 skein required

Floss Lengths

Row 1	56"
Rows 2 - 8	48"
Row 9	56"

9.
8.
7.
6.
5.
4.
3.
2.
1.

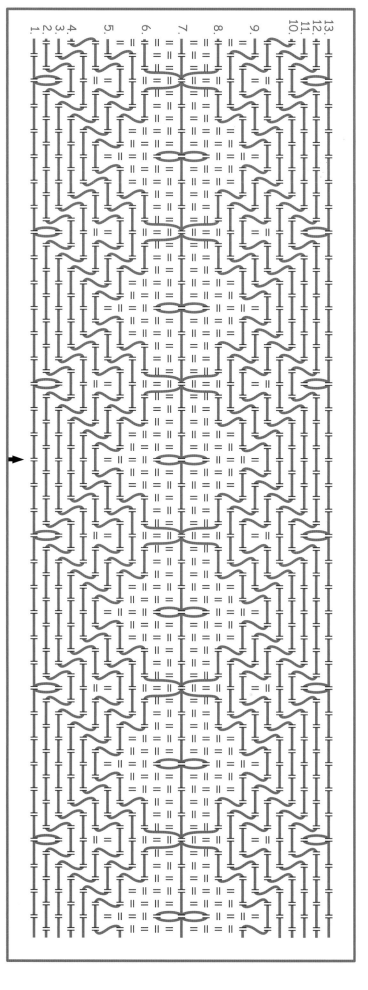

Floss Lengths

Rows 1 - 3	32"
Rows 4 - 5	40"
Row 6	48"
Row 7	40"
Row 8	48"
Rows 9 - 10	40"
Rows 11 - 13	32"

▭ DMC 743 — 2 skeins required

Read General Instructions, pgs. 2-4, before beginning project. Continue stitching in established pattern to edges of towel.

13.
12.
11.
10.
9.
8.
7.
6.
5.
4.
3.
2.
1.

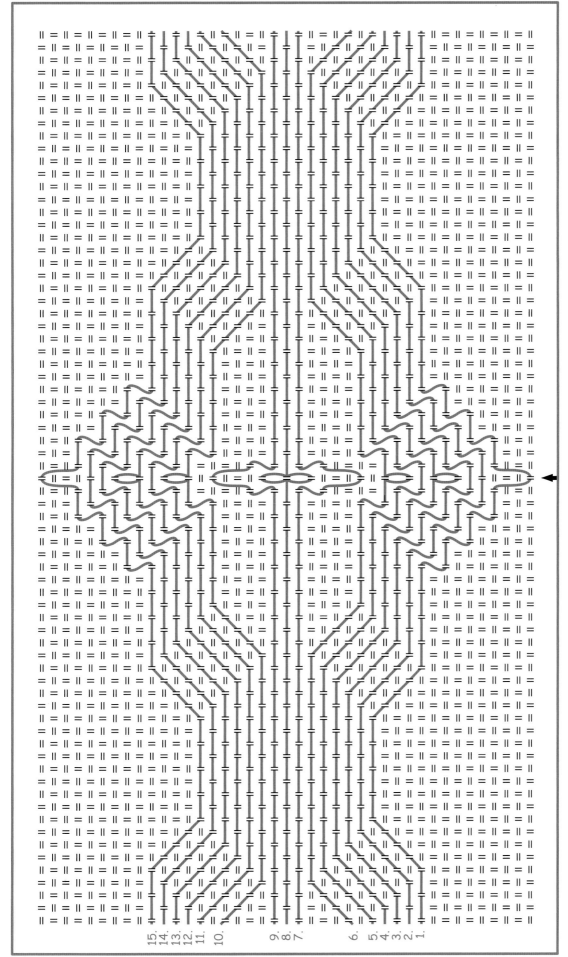

15.
14.
13.
12.
11.
10.

9.
8.
7.

6.
5.
4.
3.
2.
1.

━━ DMC 798 — 2 skeins required

Read General Instructions, pgs. 2-4, before beginning project. Continue stitching in established pattern to edges of towel.

Floss Lengths
Rows 1 - 15   40"

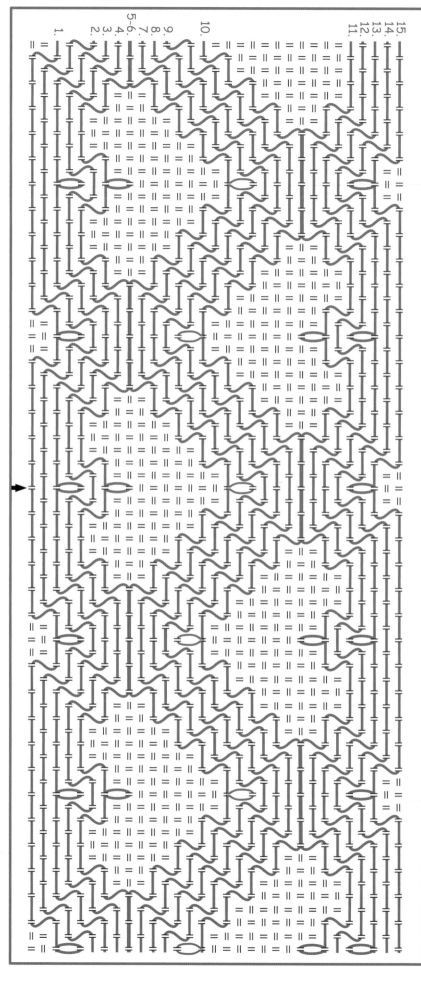

DMC 798 — 3 skeins required

Floss Lengths
Rows 1 - 5   40"
Rows 6 - 10   48"
Rows 11 - 15   40"

Read *General Instructions*, pgs. 2-4, before beginning project. Continue stitching in established pattern to edges of towel.

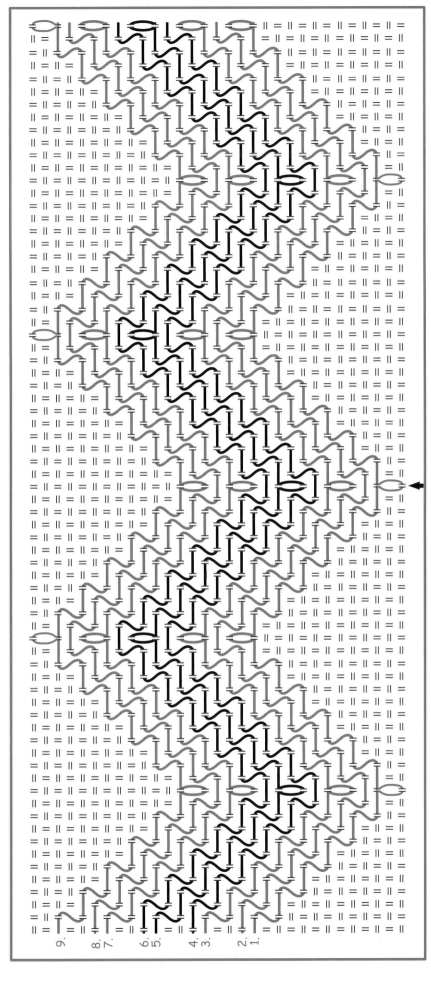

Read General Instructions, pgs. 2-4, before beginning project. Continue stitching in established pattern to edges of towel.

DMC 798 — 2 skeins required
DMC 799 — 1 skein required

Floss Lengths
Row 1   64"
Rows 2 - 8   56"
Row 9   64"

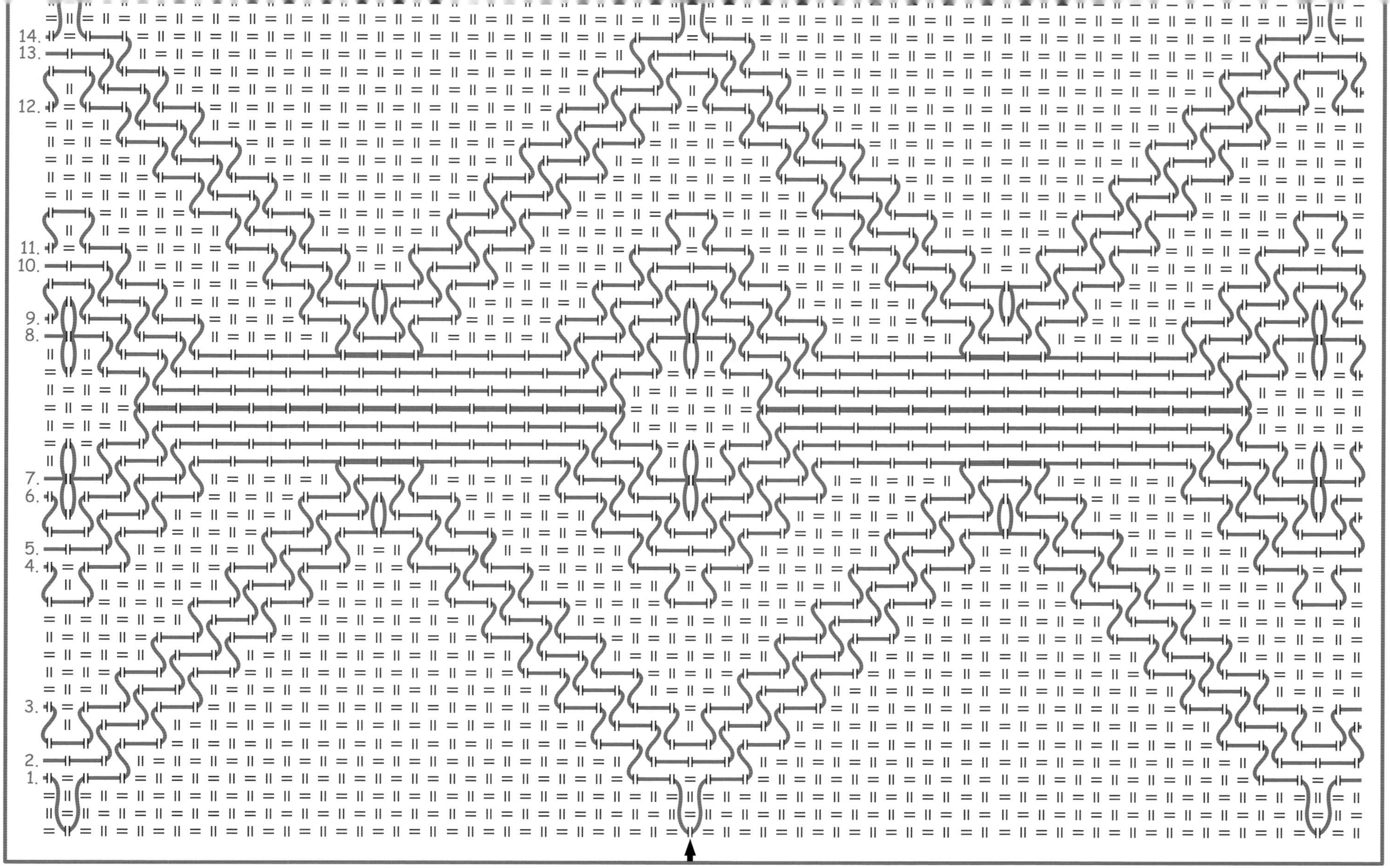

DMC 798 — 3 skeins required

Floss Lengths

Row 1	56"
Rows 2 - 3	48"
Rows 4 - 11	40"
Rows 12 - 13	48"
Row 14	56"

Read General Instructions, pgs. 2-4, before beginning project. Continue stitching in established pattern to edges of towel.

16.
15.
14.
13.
12.
11.
10.
9.
8.
7.
6.
5.
4.
3.
2.
1.

Read General Instructions, pgs. 2-4, before beginning project. Continue stitching in established pattern to edges of towel.

— DMC 320 — 2 skeins required

Floss Lengths

Rows 1 - 3	32"
Rows 4 - 7	40"
Rows 8 - 9	48"
Rows 10 -13	40"
Rows 14 - 16	32"

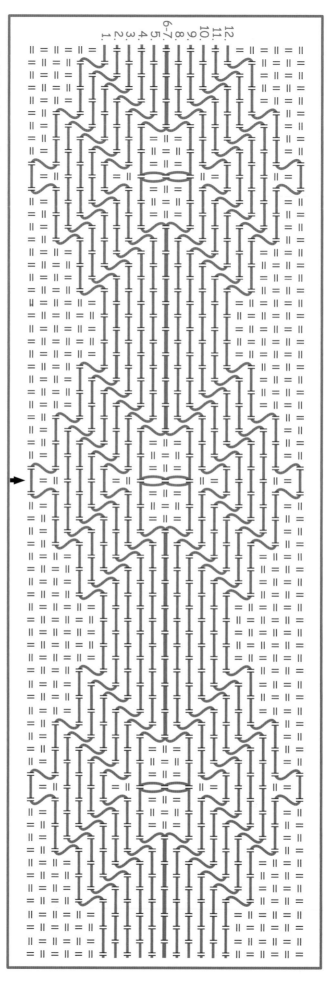

DMC 666 — 2 skeins required

Floss Lengths
Rows 1 - 12   40"

Read General Instructions, pgs. 2-4,
before beginning project. Continue
stitching in established pattern to
edges of towel.

12.
11.
10.
9.
8.
6-7.
5.
4.
3.
2.
1.

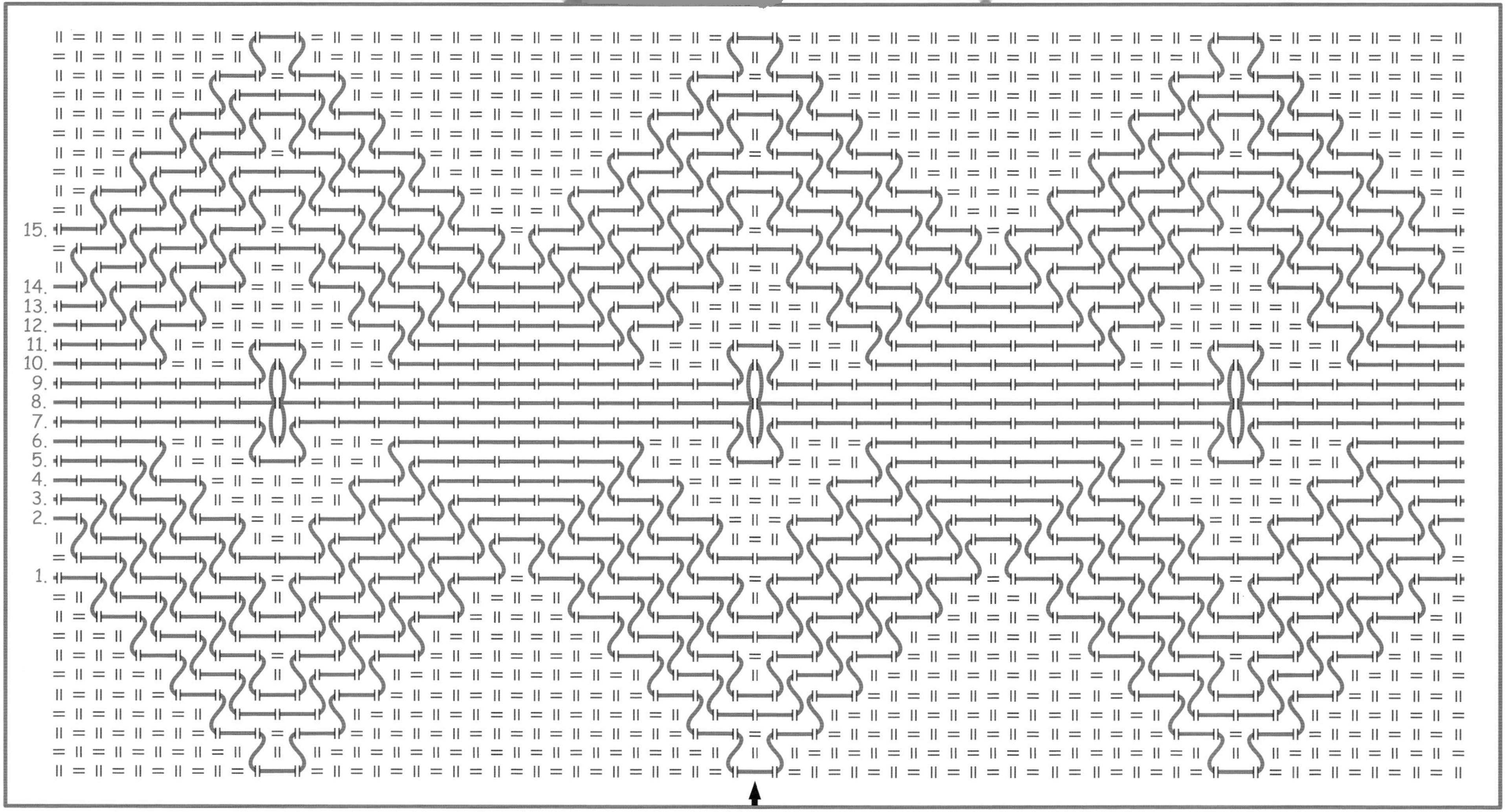

Read General Instructions, pgs. 2-4, before beginning project. Continue stitching in established pattern to edges of towel.

Floss Lengths

Rows 1 - 4	48"
Rows 5 - 6	40"
Row 7	32"
Row 8	40"
Row 9	32"
Rows 10 - 11	40"
Rows 12 - 15	48"

DMC 797 — 3 skeins required

DMC 500 — 3 skeins required

Floss Lengths
Rows 1- 14   48"

Read General Instructions, pgs. 2-4,
before beginning project. Continue
stitching in established pattern to
edges of towel.

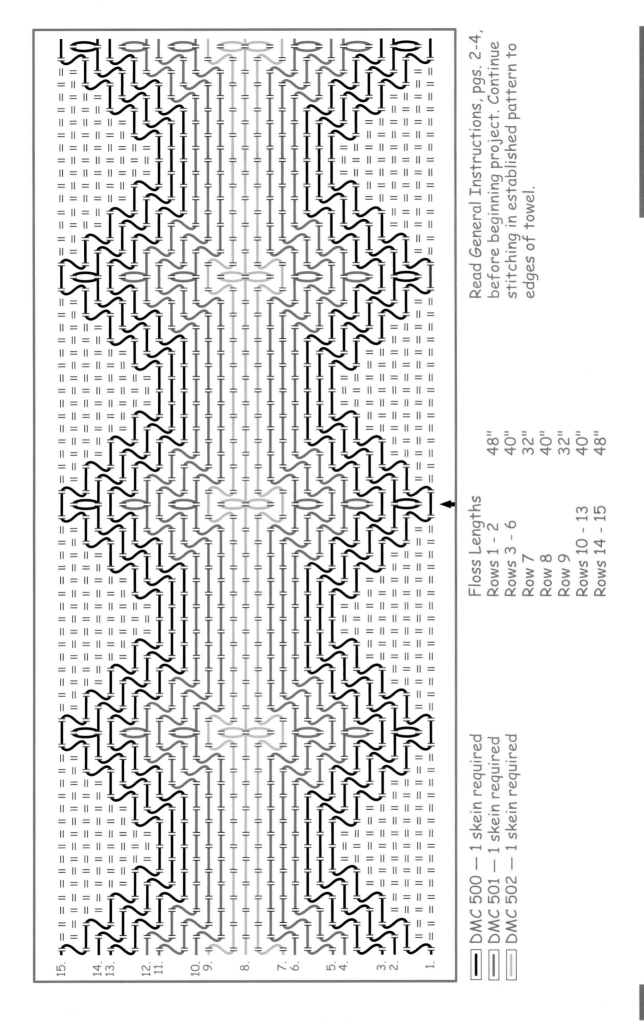

Read *General Instructions*, pgs. 2-4, before beginning project. Continue stitching in established pattern to edges of towel.

Floss Lengths

Rows 1 - 2	48"
Rows 3 - 6	40"
Row 7	32"
Row 8	40"
Row 9	32"
Rows 10 - 13	40"
Rows 14 - 15	48"

DMC 500 — 1 skein required
DMC 501 — 1 skein required
DMC 502 — 1 skein required

—— DMC 797 — 2 skeins required

Floss Lengths

Row 1	64"
Row 2	56"
Row 3	48"
Row 4	40"
Row 5	48"
Row 6	40"
Row 7	48"
Row 8	56"
Row 9	64"

Read General Instructions, pgs. 2-4, before beginning project. Continue stitching in established pattern to edges of towel.